HABITATIN' FOR HUMANITY

by William E. Chisham

Habitatin' For Humanity

Published By:
Old Red Barn Publishing
P.O. Box 921
Sequim, WA 98382, USA

Produced in the United States of America

Soft cover   ISBN: 978-0-615-26106-5

Also by the Author:

"Reflexions,": 1985-86
A Poetry Chapbook
1986

"The Road North -
Tales of An Urban Sourdough"
2006

"The Photo Op"
2008

Dedicated...

to the families and volunteers I have worked with over the years from Gresham, Oregon, to Forks, Washington, with stops in Sequim and Port Angeles, and to the wives who accept having talented husbands who don't always have the same work ethics at home.

Contents:

Introduction

One of my brother-in-laws that I see occasionally when he stops by to borrow a tool or two always asks, "Are you still habitatin' for humanity?" and I tell him about what project and what stage we are working on. He is not into volunteering because of the low pay so I try to put in a few hours for him though my carpentry skills are less than his. At least he is to be thanked for providing me with a title.

The idea behind this book is to walk through the building of a habitat house - or any house under construction - into a home from the perspective of either a homeowner-to-be or a new volunteer with little or no knowledge of house building. That person, with or without experience using basic hand tools arrives at a site and can be overwhelmed by what is happening. There is noise and organized confusion and people in worn work clothes that have seen better days. And sometimes not enough time and crew to adequately help a person come on board and understand what's happening.

This book answers some of the questions about what is going on at each stage of the project. While it is not an instruction manual, it does offer enough information to understand why some things are done the way they are. Such as why the shower enclosure is standing in the house-to-be before the walls are finished. Or why faucets are installed before the sink finds a home.

For those interested in more specific details of the parts of the process, a number of detailed references are available. The steps talked about are based on projects I have worked on and from having watched our own home being built. Habitat For Humanity has built a lot of homes all over the world. What is done out on the Olympic Peninsula in Washington State may not be the same as a rural area in an emerging nation. Proceed accordingly.

The author is a longtime Habitat volunteer i.e. grunt who has helped build twenty homes in Gresham, OR, and Sequim, Port Angeles, and Forks, WA. He feels that volunteering is a neat way to contribute to others and to meet great people and enjoy fine dining while enjoying lunch a la work site.

Bill Chisham

HABITATIN' FOR HUMANITY

In The Beginning -
A House In Site

Long before volunteers start building a Habitat house, land for a building site is needed. Cost, location, and available utilities are some of the factors considered. The land that Habitat volunteers build homes on is purchased or donated. The six homes on Maizie Court in Sequim, WA were built on land donated by Maizie Maloney. Money to purchase land comes from donations, fundraisers, and from the income stream created when the past and future homeowners make payments on their homes. If land in one area becomes too expensive, other sites are sought so that affordable homes can be built. The cost of available land in Sequim is now prohibitive so projects are being done in the Port Angeles area. One unit further away in Forks has also been completed.

The eight-unit project in Gresham, OR at 188th and Powell where I first volunteered was built on donated land that had been a vacant lot where neighbors dumped trash and drug users abandoned their needles. The property had the positive factors of being adjacent to public transportation (the MAX line), stores, and schools. Completion of the project helped revitalize the area.

The site and building costs must fit in a price range that a first time homeowner can afford. While the loan will be interest free and the mortgage may be between sixty and eighty thousand dollars, the intent is to provide adequate housing at a price that fits the budget of the new homeowner. The prospective homeowners have attended an informational meeting, filled out an application form, and gone through a selection process. They must be employed, meet financial and other guidelines, and complete other requirements. They will attend classes on becoming a homeowner and agree to work 'sweat equity' hours during the building process.

After a site is obtained, the Habitat chapter committees go through the process of planning the number of units that can be built on the site, designing the units, obtaining necessary permits, and selecting families. All this happens long before volunteer boots are on the ground to start actual work on site. A decision has been made by the construction committee as to building one house at a time or having several units underway at the same time. While this planning process goes on work is being done on any current project so that volunteers can move to a new project when the prior one is finished.

Finally it's time to break ground on the new site. The site has been cleared and leveled as necessary. String lines and stakes outline the house or houses. Survey transits are used and reused to confirm location, correct height above ground level and to make sure that the foundation forms will be level. The foundation and slab work is sometimes done by professionals to speed up the building process. Trenches are dug by hand or machine for the foundations and for the utility lines. The foundation excavations must, per local building codes, extend down past the frost line. Forms of two-by-twelve lumber or plywood panels are carefully placed in the trenches and supported by stakes. The forms are sprayed with oil on the inside to make later removal easier.

A wider area at the lower part of the wall is framed for footings that will bear the weight of the foundation. The forms are rigidly braced and wired to hold the weight of the concrete that will be poured in. Steel re-bar is cut, bent, and wire-tied together to be positioned in the forms to reinforce the foundation and footings. Then a building inspector makes an inspection for code compliance.

The process to this point is the same regardless of whether the house will be built on a slab or have floor joists over a crawl space. Finally one or more ready-mix trucks arrive on site. After backing into place, the driver lowers and extends a metal chute. With the re-bar tied in the forms and volunteers in faded cement-pour jeans and rubber boots standing armed with shovels, rakes and tamping tools, the pour is started. The rocky gray cement mix rumbles down the chute into the forms and is shoveled slowly along each wall. The forms are filled at a uniform rate to spread the weight evenly during the pour. This prevents concentration of weight that can lead to sudden 'blowouts' and frantic shoveling and extra bracing to corral the wayward mix. Tamping is done as the cement rises to make sure there are no air pockets.

As the forms are topped off and leveled with trowels, a volunteer carrying j-shaped tie-down bolts carefully places them at set intervals in the fresh cement. These bolts eventually hold down the sill or base plates which will be added after the cement cures. Unless another foundation is to be poured, it's time to clean up the tools. Work will start again when the foundation is ready for the next step.

After the foundation walls are hardened and cured and the forms removed, the project can go two ways. If a crawl space is planned under the floor, stem walls will have been poured at the same time as the foundation. Wide sill plates will be bolted down on top of the foundation, rim joists installed on top of them, joist hangers hung, and floor joists placed.

If a slab is to be poured, the area inside the foundation will be filled with a mixture of sand and rock called 'reject', and tamped down with a plate compactor several inches below the top of the foundation.

This process involves placing of stakes in the fill and adorning them with colored tape at the proper height to guide the screeding process. Or parallel metal rods may be laid to guide the screed board. Then the carefully leveled and tamped material will be dug into as plumbing and power conduit pipes are placed. The leveling and tamping will then be redone as needed.

If a house on a slab is to have radiant heating, the next step is to place a layer of plastic over the fill and thick blue board over the plastic. Radiant heating piping called 'pex' tubing is stapled on top of the blue board in looping patterns to supply the various heating zones. After this is done, cement is poured to form the slab. It is leveled carefully with very long-handled floats to smooth the surface. Jutting upward through the slab are the pipes for plumbing, electrical service, and the radiant heating. Somewhere there are squares of blueboard in the new surface. Those will be dug out later so that toilet and tub drains can be hooked up. Now the volunteers can start to build the exterior walls.

If the house is not on a slab, decking/sub-flooring is laid over the floor joists and the walls are the next step. Either way, working with top and bottom plates and two-by-six studs, the skeleton of the house slowly starts to emerge as framing starts.

A Day At A Habitat Site

Shortly before 9 a.m. the volunteers start to arrive at the building site. The number may be only four or five or up to sixteen or seventeen depending on the work to be done. Many of the regulars have worked together on various Habitat sites over four or five years. Some come one or two days every week while others come to help on specific tasks such as framing, roof truss installation or hanging cabinets. Most are retired with backgrounds ranging from skilled blue collar work through professions such as engineering, medicine, and law. The average skill level is very high though some new volunteers have no building experience and are eager to learn. Homeowners-to-be are there to put in the hours of sweat equity they are contributing.

The volunteers cluster in small groups and chat while the site supervisor hustles around looking at what was done the previous work day, what needs to be changed, and what is to be done that day. He or she may or may not have the most knowledge or professional experience in construction but is the person responsible for getting the job done quickly and safely, answering questions, assigning tasks and finding anything that can't be found. He or she also starts an hour earlier so that power cords are laid out, air compressors are ready, and work can start on time. If the weather is overly abrasive, the crew seeks shelter inside the house under construction or in the tool storage trailer. Most work days there is hot coffee and may even be a supply of donuts or leftover cookies. Brownies never last to the leftover stage.

Most of the volunteers are dressed in jeans combined with aging T-shirts, flannel shirts, sweatshirts, and baseball caps as the weather demands more or less cover. Then rain gear, work jackets, and even rubber boots are added to the blend. Comfort tops style every time. A few hardy souls sometimes defy Mother Nature with shorts.

Though the Habitat chapter supplies enough tools for everyone, there is a certain comfort level in having one's own tools to handle most of the usual tasks that will be done. A personal hammer that fits the hand wins over an off-the-shelf, one-size-fits-all clunker. The regulars and the occasional professional are more likely to bring their own tool belts or tool buckets. The tool belt pockets hold enough basic tools to save a lot of trips to the tool trailer to hunt for things like a nail set, screw driver or utility knife. And having your own cordless drill can save a lot of time looking for one not in use or finding one with a battery that needs to be charged. Hard-hats are provided for mandatory wear anytime there is work above ground level.

At times a professional carpenter, usually between jobs, will show up to volunteer. They are the guys with the heaviest and highest-mileage tool belts and are the least likely to have shaved before heading for the job site. Working with one of these pro's for a day is a non-stop education in how a house quickly gets put together. Using framing hammers that most volunteers can't lift, they can drive a sixteen-penny nail home while mere mortals are just setting one in place. When a professional finish carpenter is on site to install stairs, window ledges, and cabinets, we are suitably awed by the precision and accuracy of the results. We do good work but not quite that good!

Around 9 a.m. the site supervisor rounds up the crew, introduces any new volunteers to the oldies, and gives a brief talk about site safety. Don't use power tools such as nail guns and saws unless you are qualified and checked out on them. Don't slip on ice, trip over power cords, or fall. Make sure ladders are placed properly. New volunteers sign a liability release form before starting work and are given a set of safety rules. Then jobs are assigned to teams of two or three and to individuals. These assignments may be changed often during the day depending on tasks being completed, skill level needed, priority, who shows up later, and who leaves early. As in baseball, being able to play any position helps.

At this point what appears to be organized chaos seems to rule. Hard hats and tool belts are put on. More power cords are being laid out, air compressor lines are hooked to tools, and work stations are set up for power saws, painting, siding cutting or whatever is planned for the day. Suddenly the scene shifts as work gets started on everything from siding to roofing to moving dirt.

Somewhere around noon a lunch provided by a church group or other volunteers arrives. The noise of the saws, nail guns, and air compressors stops as a welcome break is taken. Every lunch is good but the regular volunteers keep an eye out for the arrival of those that have a reputation for being extra special. Such as a hearty chicken soup or barbeque beef sloppy Joe's accompanied by homemade brownies for dessert. Politics and local news are bandied about during the meal. Who's not there and why is covered. Then back to work till 3:30 or 4 p.m. when it's time to clean up the site, put the tools away, and head for home. It's one more day forward toward a completed home.

Belting Up And Tooling Around The Job Site: Are Carpenters Square?

A first time walk-on volunteer with little or no prior building experience is not likely to show up wearing a weathered and worn tool belt or carrying a bucket of tools. Even some of the most experienced volunteers rely on the on-site tools and tool belts provided by the Habitat Chapter and found somewhere in the construction trailer or shed. (Rule: Put it away at the end of the day where it came from - or on the table out front so that someone else can return it to where it came from.) If a newbie does show up with a tool belt, the impression is that he or she is well experienced till proven otherwise.

To avoid repeated trips to the tool storage area somewhere near the coffee pot, I prefer my own tool belt, tool bucket, and cordless drill. That way I have the gear to perform most routine tasks and don't have to worry about some tools being in use elsewhere on busy days. Or find that a battery for a cordless drill needs to be charged. If I pass the point of doing a task with what I have, the tool shelves in the storage trailer are where I might be able to find the special tool that I need. It's also the place where I will find the correct nails, screws, or other supplies for the project of the day.

A typical tool belt might be loaded with some of the following things:

Medium-weight claw hammer hung in a loop on the right or left side. Some of the pro's carry them in a fixture at the rear center of a deluxe belt that may even be supported by suspenders. The rear hammer location is better when ladder descending.

Tape measure in a center pouch over the navel area. This tool is used almost as much as the hammer and hopefully with the same accuracy.

Speed square.

Nail set in one of the narrow slots over the hammer loop.

Flat carpenter's pencil (sharpened) in another of the narrow slots.

Utility knife to sharpen the pencil, score drywall, and so on.

Screwdriver, reversible between Phillip's head and flat blade screws.

Nails and screws from prior projects.

Five-way scraper/putty knife/etc.

Miscellaneous items carried from time to time are a stud finder, work gloves, channel lock pliers, cat's paw pry bar, drywall saw, and chalk line. Otherwise, those items stay in a tool bucket in the car or near where I am working. Also in the bucket is my combination square, safety glasses, ear protection, small hand saw, dead blow hammer, small sledge hammer, drill bits, work gloves, pry bars, drywall lifter, bevel gauge, and rasp. Also, a supply of band aids to patch up the occasional blood flow from minor scrapes. Most of the tools are marked with my name and telephone number so that they can find the way home if loaned out or lost or left behind at the end of the day.

Site and Sight Safety

The only routine part of a day working at a Habitat site, aside from coffee and lunch, is the safety briefing that is part of the morning muster. Repetition of basic concepts does seem to hold the on-site injury rate down as more volunteers seem to injure themselves doing at home projects then on Habitat work days. Such as one experienced friend who damaged a finger at home trying to stop a router bit. So to repeat in more detail what was said earlier:

Wear a hard hat unless told by the site supervisor that work is at a stage where it is not mandatory. That is not often. Even working inside, it's easy to climb a ladder and hit a truss or beam with the top of your head. Or to be bonked by a tool that falls off the ladder and should have not been left up there. A cordless drill that falls from the top of a step ladder may miss hitting anyone but can suffer fatal damage when it lands.

Let's face it: not everyone, male or female, looks good in a hard hat. Certainly not like the macho males on construction crews in TV ads and programs. And, in real time, the hats have a habit of falling off if one leans back to look up at what might be falling or bends forward to pick up a dropped tool or whatever else fell. Yet rules are rules and this one is firm. Any time things are going on above eye level, wear one. They are provided for you and all you have to do is figure out how to adjust them to stay on.

Safety glasses are another item that is provided. They are to be worn anytime that dust or other airborne material such as sawdust or flying wood scraps can get in your eyes. Cutting wood, HardiePlank™, or composite materials such as particle board raises a scenic cloud of airborne debris that seek eyes to irritate or otherwise injure. The stuff floating around is not always just pure sawdust. It may have more chemicals in it than some supermarket items.

Along with eye protection, hear what your ears are fighting. There is often an air compressor going full tilt, nail guns being fired, power saws going on and off, hammers being exercised, and the shop vac passing by. Ear plugs or other hearing protectors should be used more than they are.

Related to eye and ear protection is foot care. Sandals are a no-no and even tennis shoes are marginal for comfort and safety. Good work boots with steel toes are the ideal safe way to go. They protect against falling objects, nail punctures, and twisted ankles from walking around a sometimes less than level job site.

Ladder safety is another biggie. Ladders must be set level, not leveled with scrap lumber, and extension ladders must be at the correct distance and angle from the wall.

Stay off of the top of step ladders. If in doubt, ask for help in holding the ladder. Don't lean back to the point where gravity takes charge. When stepping off of a ladder, be sure you are at the bottom step.

Power tools are another quick way to earn an instant injury. Any volunteer using them must be qualified and cleared by the site supervisor. Nails guns are mostly air powered and can fire a sixteen-penny nail through a two-by-four to nail it to another one. Or tie a foot to a roof deck if pointed the wrong way. Or fire through a sheet of siding if the stud is missed. The bump and shoot feature is disabled but might not be. Don't have a finger on the trigger unless ready to fire. And understand that a nail can hit a knot in the wood and angle out where the shooter is holding the pieces together. If the gun jams, disconnect the air supply before trying to clear the jam.

Table saws, circular saws, and chop saws are another fertile field for ways to get hurt. The basic concept is to not bring fingers and other essential body parts in contact with the moving - or stationary - saw blade. They're sharp! Don't get in a contorted position and try to operate a saw cross-handed. Support long boards with stands or call for help holding the far end. After making a cut, freeze in place until the saw blade has stopped completely. If the saw guard doesn't work, stop and call for help. Unplug the saw before changing a blade. Know that a skill saw can kick back in use and become eleven pounds of live action with your finger still on the trigger. Material being fed through a table saw incorrectly can kick back at crotch level so never stand behind the material being pushed through. Cut off material can be propelled toward the person on the far side of the saw. Use a push stick rather than fingers. Follow the rule of never cutting a small piece narrower than the blade diameter.

Just navigating around the site is another challenge. Air and power cords are here and there. Ditches spring up around the area to stumble into. Ice is a factor at times. Cross braces inside and out can test the sturdiness of your hard hat. Nails in scrap lumber that were not pulled out as instructed can impale body parts. Hammers that contact finger nails instead of building nails can cause impact damage.

If working above the ground such as on a roof, a safety harness is worn to catch you if you fall off the roof. The time of hanging in space in the harness is easier to endure than the impact with the ground or a stack of lumber.

Finally, remember to lift properly or get help. Use the knees rather than the back. Don't try to carry all the lumber for a wall at one time. Or try to move three sixty-pound sacks of ready mix in one trip. Even though your chiropractor may appreciate the business.

Our affiliate has a written safety pamphlet given to all new volunteers for reading and heeding. The message in all this is not to discourage or frighten but to raise the awareness level. Think safety and leave work at the end of the day rather than exit early to seek medical attention. As I, the oracle, have had to do.

Wood We?

After the foundation and slab are finished, or when floor joists are to be installed, large piles of lumber seem to materialize around the site. They arrive on a large truck, are dropped off, and are moved closer to the work area by us. The pieces will be moved again as they are used or for other reasons. A person new to a building site might be totally confused by the size, length, and width of the stuff in the various piles. What goes where? How can all this be sorted, measured, cut, and made into a house? A few basic concepts can help sort out some of the confusion.

Much of the stuff falls into the sobriquet of dimension lumber. A lot of it is likely to be Douglas Fir. The length can be from ninety-two-and-five-eighths-inches for wall studs to sixteen feet or longer for plates and joists. Width can range from four-inches-or-less to twelve-inches-or-more depending where it is headed. Thickness can be from three-quarter-inch-or-less up to four-inches-or-more if for a support post or beam. Of course those numbers are not the true width or thickness unless the wood is rough cut rather than

finished. Therefore four inches becomes three-and-one
-half inches, one inch is three-quarter-inch, two inches
is one-and-one-half inches and so forth. Which means
that a two-by-six is really one-and-one-half-inches
thick and five-and-one-half-inches wide. Five-quarters
material is a true one inch thick. An exterior wall
framed with two-by-sixes is really five-and-one-half-
inches wide before adding interior drywall plus exterior
sheathing, blueboard, and siding. Don't fret, just do, as
the designer has allowed for all this. Just accept that
an eight-foot two-by-four or two-by-six stud is ninety-
two-and-five-eighths-inches long so that it won't need
cutting to length. At least if it is stamped 'stud.'

Another clue to watch for is the wood color.
Some of it seems to look reddish or darker. It also has
marks on it that make it look like it has been through a
meat tenderizer. This is pressure-treated lumber
which has been subjected to a special process to inject
it with a preservative. Though current methods make it
not as unsafe as prior methods, gloves are worn when
handling it. This wood is destined for any place down
low where dampness of cement meets wood (think sill
plates, base plates or interior wall bottom plates) or
for fence posts where dirt is involved.

Then there are the four-by-eight-foot sheets that
look like they are made of wood chips. They are. The
layers of chips are 'oriented' into a specific direction in
each layer to make the panel stronger. Therefore it is
called oriented strand board or 'OSB'. The thickness
may vary depending on intended use such as for

exterior sheathing, roof decking, or floor decking. There may also be real plywood (made of wood plies pressure glued together) on site for use on counter tops. Then there is other non-wood wood that arrives along the way such as melamine shelving or composite baseboard trim along with special wood for special places.

For best building results, most of the dimension lumber needs to be sorted into three piles: good, usable, and return to sender. Terms like crown, curl, bow, cup, and wave describe the variations from straight along the length and width. The worst pieces are obvious even to the untrained eye and will be returned or cut into shorter pieces for use in blocking or where defects are less critical. A sorter eyeballs down the length of the board and uses chalk to mark a bow or a wow. Undetected defects can make door and window openings less than square. Or walls that pooch in or out when drywall or siding is installed. In any event, the piles of material will disappear as they morph into a finished house.

Framed

    After the slab is finished, framing the house can finally begin. Fifteen or twenty volunteers arrive ready to start on the bones of the new building. The trenches around the foundation have had gutter drain pipe, conduit for electrical service, and water and sewer lines laid in them over gravel and backfilling done by machine if one is available. Otherwise shovels and wheelbarrows and muscles get the job done. Now seen lurking around the site are stacks of OSB (oriented-strand board) sheathing, stacks of long two-by-six lumber, piles of two-by-fours, and wall studs in two widths. As drivers do not unload material close to the slab, the first task is to move the piles closer to the work area. Lumber does not move on its own unless gravity is involved. For an hour or so lifting, walking, and stacking skills are honed.

    While this is done, other workers are using the house plans to locate and snap red chalk lines on the slab. The lines mark where the exterior and interior walls will be placed and doors and windows will be located. The snapped lines are sometimes sprayed with a preservative to weatherproof them. Two-by-six pressure-treated lumber is cut and placed flat along the chalk lines inside the perimeter to make a 'sill plate' or 'base plate' where the wood meets the concrete. That is, a sill plate can also be a base plate or there can be one of each.

Which term applies depends on the method of construction. If the exterior walls are prefabricated ahead of time with a base plate, they may then be moved on to the slab and placed over a sill plate of pressure-treated lumber. If exterior walls are not made ahead of time, the sill plate and base plate may be the same single piece of pressure-treated lumber. Otherwise, an untreated two-by-six 'base plate' is stacked on top of each piece of pressure-treated sill plate. The pieces are temporarily fastened together with two-headed 'duplex' nails. Using a carpenter's square, the location of each hold-down bolt is transferred to the center of the pieces and holes drilled through them before separating the boards.

After sweeping drilling debris away, the sill plates, if used, are placed over the hold-down bolts above a blue weatherproofing material. The volunteers now form teams to work on the wall sections. Two-by-six top 'upper plates' are placed next to the base plates which have holes drilled to go over the hold down bolts. Both plates are then measured and marked with 'IX' symbols to show sixteen-inch 'on-center' locations for the vertical studs. Door and window openings are marked during this step. The openings are usually wider than the sixteen inches and interfere with the logical marking process. Places where interior walls will join the exterior walls are indicated for extra studs.

The studs are carried over from the place where they were stacked earlier. They go vertically between the base plate and the top plate usually on sixteen-inch -centers. The process gets more like a card game as 'kings', 'jacks', 'cripples', and 'headers' enter the playing field. A 'king stud' is used top to bottom at the sides of each opening. Inboard of each king stud is a 'jack stud' which is face nailed to the king stud with sixteen-penny nails. The nails are slightly angled so that they will not extend out the far side.

The jack studs are cut shorter to support a horizontal piece between the bordering kings as part of a 'header' over door and window openings. This opening will be filled with two-by-twelve or other material as further support. Below window openings, one or two horizontal pieces are placed. They are supported by 'cripples' from the lower side to the top of the base plate. The wall is completed by adding studs at right angles at each end to meet the end of the joining wall.

After all the wall pieces are laid out on the slab, they are nailed together by hammer or nail gun. No one picks up or operates a nail gun unless cleared by the site supervisor. The wall is first checked for square by diagonal corner-to-corner measurements. This is called 'running the corners' though it does not involve actual running. As several walls may be underway at the same time, the groups of volunteers compete for the available space on the slab. Lunch break will be the time to crow about who got their wall done first.

Exterior sheathing may be added at this point to keep the wall square while it is raised into place. It is easier to sheath the entire wall while it is still down but wall weight and number of lifters is considered. A thirty -four-foot wall covered with OSB can be a challenge. The site supervisor calls for all volunteers to come and help lift the wall. The goal is to lift it up to but not past ninety degrees. It must end up fitting over the hold-down bolts and meet the adjacent wall. Scrap wood is placed under the bottom edge to get some initial height and under the top to allow finger space for the lifters.

The lifting process involves bringing the wall to knee level first and then everyone trying to lift at the same rate while walking the wall up to vertical and setting it over the hold-down bolts which will then have large washers and bolts put on. Going past ninety degrees is a no-no especially on an upper level. No one is to let go and walk away before the wall is up, secured in place, and braced. A sixteen-pound sledge hammer is used to coax the wall into place fore and aft and next to the chalk line. Bracing is added to support each section while other sections are built and lifted. Each wall raised seems to add to the momentum of the workers.

When all the exterior walls are in place, string lines offset outside along the wall are used to check for end-to-end wall straightness. If the slab is level and square, this process goes a lot easier. Bows in or out are corrected and braced. Interior walls are built using pressure-treated lumber for the bottom plate and raised. Most use two-by-four material except for load-bearing walls or those with plumbing pipes running through them which use two-by-six material. Diagonals are run to verify squareness before top tie plates are added over all the walls. Each wall section is checked for plumb before it is secured to the slab using a ram set to drive a special nail into the slab using a .22 caliber cartridge. Hearing protection is required. If a second floor is to be built, rim and floor joists are added before floor decking is laid above the lower floor and the framing process repeated.

When the walls are up, braced, and squared, it's show time as prefabricated roof trusses arrive at the site. The longest ones span the house plus two feet on either side so the trailer and crane truck towing it are a long combination. Most of the volunteers sit or stand back at this stage and watch the show. Two or three agile workers are on the top of the house frame to guide the trusses as they are lifted to the top of the frame. A worker on the ground holds a tether rope tied to the truss as it is lifted and swung from trailer to frame top. Several stacks are soon lying across the house frame. The truck departs and work proceeds as the show is over.

The trusses are carefully raised to vertical one at a time. Each is moved forward into place and nailed down. They are set up twenty-two-and-one-half-inches apart which makes them twenty-four-inches on-center.

Long one-by-four boards are used to space and brace them. Shorter trusses may be used to form sections at angles to the main roof. The difficult part is fitting any pieces that meet at forty-five degrees to run out to the house corner to form a gable roof.

Two-by-four 'bird blocks' twenty-two-and-one-half -inches long are placed on edge on top of the framing between the trusses. That explains the pile of short two-by-four pieces that came with the trusses. The truss ends are framed with long horizontal two-by-four 'barge boards' or 'sub-fascia' around the house that help form the eaves which may or may not be enclosed. One-by-six pre-primed fascia is added over this.

If the house does not have end trusses at right angles to the cross trusses, lookouts are needed to carry the roof forward enough at the front and back to create an overhang. This is done by notching the two trusses at each end of the house so that two-by-fours can be laid in and extended past the ends of the house. Sub-fascia and fascia are nailed to the outboard end of these pieces. Four-foot-by-eight-foot roof decking is laid down on the trusses, trimmed to fit, spaced, and nailed.

Hurricane clip ties are nailed to hold the trusses to the top plates using fat 'Tico™' nails. The bottom of each truss now becomes the rafter that will hold the ceiling drywall in place. As the placement of the interior walls conflicts in many places with this logical order, two-by-six boards are used to top the walls lengthwise to make a nailing surface for the drywall.

The next step is to nail sheathing onto the exterior walls, if this was not done earlier, following a code-prescribed nailing pattern with galvanized nails used on the lower edge. As a final step, sturdy metal tie-downs are screwed on inside of each corner of the house over the bolts that anchor the sill plate and bottom plate down. Over a few work days, volunteers have combined nails and lumber into what now looks almost like a house.

An Ex-Siding Time

As the OSB sheathing is completed, the door and window openings are cut out using a reciprocating saw or a router with a special bit. Then a framing inspection is called for. It's times like that when any framing errors come to light. Such as when a crew of professional framers volunteered but forgot to frame out a window. Sheathing off, framing redone, sheathing back on. Or when a stress panel is forgotten and the sheathing does not extend in one four-foot piece from each corner.

Now the crew has a chance to use the stacks of blueboard (one-or-two-inch thick, two-foot-by-eight-foot Styrofoam panels donated by Dow) to cover the sheathing. These will be nailed in place with long roofing nails capped with bright orange or green washers that keep them from sinking below the panel surface. The nails, if dropped, tend to sit upright and seek shoe soles to poke through. Any needed cutting of the board is done with a small hand saw, sheet rock saw, or on the table saw. The board, being light, goes up quickly. The seams are taped for weather proofing with a special tape also made by Dow. Door and window openings are again trimmed out.

Before the siding can be installed, more prep work needs to be done. The soffits under the eaves between the walls and the barge (fascia) boards need to have material (Hardie*Soffit*™) panels perforated for venting fitted into place. Another team is busy putting up trim at each corner of the house. These one-inch-by -four-inch-by-eight-foot pre-primed pieces are nailed edgewise forming an 'L' shape. Normally half the boards are three-inches wide and the other half four-inches wide. When you look at the outside surface after installation, each board appears to be equal in width. If not ordered (or delivered) this way, then one-half of the boards will need to be ripped to width on the table saw before being used to make the dimensions equal on each side of the corner

Now, can siding start? No. Marks must be made to show where the top of each piece will line up. A 'story pole' marked with increments indicating siding width minus overlap is placed vertically alongside each corner trim piece and the marks transferred to the wall. Then a chalk line is stretched end to end along the wall between the marks at each level and a line is snapped. This will guide the top of each piece of siding and hopefully keep it level. In theory, the siding will match at each corner around the house. Vertical lines showing stud locations are then marked on the blueboard where nails will secure the siding.

We are still not done with the prep work. One-inch lengthwise ledger strips of the siding or other material must be cut and placed around the house at the lower edge of the OSB and blue board. This strip will 'kick out' the lower edge of the first row of siding to match the overlap as higher pieces are installed.

Now are we ready for the siding? Not yet. The window and door openings need something for the siding to butt up against. For the windows, it is trim cut from pre-primed one-inch-by-four-inch wood. For the doors it will be the door jambs and brick molding. Door installation is usually assigned to one or more experienced volunteers as it requires skill and extreme patience. The goal is to start with a square opening and a square door and determine why they do not fit easily. Tapered shims are inserted at various spots from each side to bring the hinge side to vertical. Then shimming of the lock side is tried. Before the jamb is finally nailed or screwed in place, the door is mounted onto the hinges. It must properly and tightly close with equal reveals around the top and sides. If not, back to the shims and levels. The jamb must also fit evenly in the door opening and not lean forward or back. After the exterior doors are properly fitted, mortising of door hardware openings will be done and construction locks installed. Now the house can be locked and some of the heavier tools can be stored inside rather than locked up in the storage trailer between work days.

Before the window trim is placed, the openings must be weatherproofed with special sticky tape and special drain mesh at the bottom. Doing all of this leads to installation of the windows before cutting and nailing the trim. The windows must be centered in the opening, leveled, and nailed following the instructions about nail placement. This is a three-person task as one person keeps the window from falling out, another person inside does leveling, centering, and bottom shimming, while the third is ready to nail. When installed, the window should open and close without binding and not have a visible light gap when closed. Drip flashing is placed along the top and bottom edges of the trim to meet the siding as it is installed.

The siding we use for the house is 'HardiePlank™', a cement and fiber material that comes in twelve-foot lengths. Each piece is carried carefully on edge as it can bend and break if mishandled. It is pre-primed but not painted the final house color. We are using an eight -inch width with a three-quarter-inch overlap which gives a seven-and-one-quarter-inch 'reveal' or visible area. The installation instructions as to spacing at each end and between pieces vary from time to time. Caulking ends and vertical seams can be done as you go or later. Seam-sealing tape should be used under the vertical seams for protection.

Finally we are underway with the siding. The bottom piece is placed, top edge matched to the chalk line, checked for level and a one-eighth-inch gap at the trim end to allow for expansion, and air-nailed into place. Two or three people are needed to do this effectively. Looking at the chalk line straight on and holding the material firmly makes for a better job. The last piece in the row is cut to length using special electric shears. Saw cutting is possible but requires a special blade and dust protection. The next row runs the opposite direction with no vertical seams close to each other and leaving a one-eighth-inch gap between ends or as otherwise instructed.

All goes well on the march up the wall until a door or window opening is encountered when precise measuring and cutting must be done to frame the opening. This is tricky because measurements from the top down need to be subtracted from the total width and the result measured up from the bottom edge. Or down from the top edge. Finally the top piece is trimmed to fit under the soffit and wood trim cut to length and nailed in place. Then on to the next wall. Two days of actual siding work can finish the average house though it doesn't always work that way.

While many of the volunteers are busy with the siding, another group of workers has been busy up on the roof. Metal drip edging has been nailed down around the edge of the roof decking and over the top of the fascia. The roof decking is covered with roofing paper which overlaps and is stapled down. This is used in place of the heavy black material that was previously used. A starter course cut from full shingles is nailed around the perimeter of the roof to help in water runoff before the full shingles are laid.

Bundles of shingles are staged on the roof using a conveyor belt from the delivery truck or carried up using a ladder. The exposed surface of each twelve-inch-by-thirty-six-inch asphalt shingle has a colored mineral layer that will provide weather protection. The underside has an adhesive band that will stick to the preceding row. Before the shingles are laid, or at the latest, during the shingling process, holes will be cut from the inside of the house at various places for vent pipes, exhaust vents, and attic vents. These are carefully installed and sealed to keep water out.

A full shingle starter course is nailed down at the lower edge of the roof with the following courses laid in a precise pattern to allow proper overlap of rows and offset of seams from row to row. Along ridges, the shingles are trimmed and later capped with shingles cut smaller. Valleys have metal flashing cut to fit under the shingles to channel water off of the roof. At this point the house looks much like an unpainted version of what it will be when finished. Yet there are miles to go before it is a home.

Dining Al Fresco

Napoleon or General von Claueswitz, or perhaps it was George Patton, once said that an army moves on its' stomach. It was not a reference to crawling on the ground. Like in an army, lunch is an essential part of the Habitat experience. It fuels the troops after an arduous morning of hard work and can even inspire them to harder work during the afternoon.

While not all Habitat chapters provide lunch, it is the time of day when the workers on site - volunteers and homeowners-to-be and family members - are all together at one time. They are not off somewhere working as part of a team or on an individual project. It's the time when saws, hammers, nail guns and air compressors fall silent. It's time to take off the tool belt and hard hat, put down the paint brush, and see what the lunch ladies and gentlemen have brought to fuel us for the rest of the day.

When I volunteered in Gresham, OR, lunch was not usually provided. Donuts at 10:30 and 2:30

coffee breaks, yes; lunch, no, on most work days. If no food magically appeared, four or five of us would traipse off-site to find a neighborhood place over on Powell. Sometimes it would be the small taqueria just around the corner. The price was right, the food was authentic, not from a chain operation, and English was a second language. Other times we would cross Powell and the MAX tracks to head for a chain burger place a block away. The hope was always that after a year the place finally had their malt machine fixed. On special occasions, such as finishing a unit, we would go to the full-service Chinese restaurant on the corner near the project and enjoy table and chair luxury.

When lunch was provided on site, it sometimes included an ethnic dish prepared by a future homeowner. On those more formal occasions, our patio dining would be seats artfully arranged on whatever pile of lumber was the right height. Or on a small entry porch if the house was that far along.

When I started volunteering in Sequim in 2003, it was a surprise to learn that lunch was provided on Wednesdays and Saturdays by volunteers from various churches in the community. Many times the menu would be homemade or store deli sandwiches, chips, soft drinks, and a dessert. Hot soup or chili on the colder days were always warmly greeted. And the Dungeness Valley (Clallam County) affiliate even has chairs to sit on. The arrival of the lunch would be imminent when the chairs were unstacked and sat in a circle on an almost level area away from the wind and rain and wasps. In really bad weather we would sit inside the house if it was at a point where it provided some shelter.

The site leader bees tended to cluster where they could discuss work progress and who had to run to get what material after lunch. The rest of us would discuss who wasn't there and why, fishing results, sailing news, and, as a last resort, politics. The conversations usually lasted until the food was gone and it was certain no more was arriving. This was difficult on the day that the lunch ladies were off-schedule and four lunches arrived in succession.

Of course as most of the volunteers have been exposed to military service, comments were sometimes made about the food. Cheese in the sandwich or no cheese. The bread or the filling. And never anything adverse said about the dessert. Soon we were gathered by our leaders and advised that such comments were being adversely received by the lunch bringers and could lead to less lunches. If you can't say something nice....

Of course some of the lunch providers did such an outstanding job that their scheduled days were looked forward to. Such as when John Glover and his wife were on tap. His large pot of hearty chicken soup with wide homemade noodles and fresh baked bread was a culinary high point. And, of course, Pat Chambers, wife of our former executive director, always received accolades for her homemade chili and corn bread.

The high point of Habitat dining locally was reached during the 2006 Blitz Build at the Campbell Avenue project. With volunteers as helpers, crews provided by area contractors rushed to complete one home in one week working day and night. Meals and snacks were provided by some of the best local eateries. Prime Rib for dinner one evening kept the work wheels turning. With such incentives it is even possible to drywall, tape, texture, and paint at night. Though one attic crawl space entry got covered over and had to be searched for the next day.

Then there are the pizza days when no group was scheduled or forgot to come. The site supervisor or someone from the affiliate office would show up bearing food from Tail Gate Pizza or Domino's. When the last brownie or cookie is consumed, the chairs are re-stacked, tool belts picked up, and back to being a home maker.

Inside
Edition

What we see from the street at this point looks like a house with siding, windows, doors, a shingled roof, painting going on, and maybe even some preliminary landscaping. The gutter people have stopped by and installed gutters and downspouts. Sidewalks, porches, and a parking area may be poured and finished. What we see if we go inside is more rudimentary. The interior walls are framed and top-plated together. Bracing that has been run into over the past few work days has mostly been removed. Hopefully all the nails were removed from it. The framing at the bottom of each door opening has been cut out using a hand saw or reciprocating saw. Now we start a number of steps that lead up to covering the walls with drywall.

At this point most of going forward depends on whether the plumbers and electricians have stopped by to do their part. Vertical black vent pipes and copper or flexible plastic water pipe plus holes and cut places in the framing are a sign that the plumbers have passed through. Holes drilled in studs and plates and electrical wire running through the holes is a clue that electrical work has happened. Another sign would be that blue plastic outlet and wall switch boxes have appeared on the studs in great profusion and the wire ends are poking out of them. Where a nail or screw could damage the wire, metal plates are in place. If the plumbing and electrical has been inspected and approved, drywalling is almost ready to start.

This is the point where someone will look my direction and say, 'Attic access openings.' which is a minor specialty for me. The house may not have a true usable attic but the space between the ceiling and the underside of the roof needs to be accessible in one or more places. Such as for 'blowing in' insulation when there is ceiling drywall to hold it in. The access is made by nailing a thirty-inch-long-by-sixteen-inch-high piece of OSB to a rafter at an appropriate location. Two pieces of two-by-four go between the rafters and another piece of OSB matches the first one. End pieces are cut and nailed onto the two-by-fours at each end and the task is done. The opening is high enough to hold the insulation in but not so high that it's impossible to enter the attic space.

Next are the 'rat boards.' These are long pieces of scrap one-by-four or other lumber nailed side by side on the rafters out from the access opening. The idea is to have something to stand on while blowing in the insulation to the far corners of the attic or to crawl on while doing other work. Walking on the drywall is not recommended.

A related task at this stage is to frame in and mount the bathroom exhaust fan and whole house fan boxes. Flexible tubing connects these to their roof vents. By this time other roof vents have been installed. And a crew has been placing heavy paper forms between the rafters down to the top plates to allow attic ventilation after the insulation is blown in.

The next task before the drywalling gets underway is to install blocking. This is done with short pieces of two-by-four and two-by-six off the scrap pile. The idea is to have a block nailed in place between the studs wherever something will be nailed or screwed in place. Each counter, vanity, upper and lower cabinet, or bathroom fixture will have an unseen piece of wood behind it to support it. The closets may have pieces for shelf-supporting ledger boards to be nailed to.

When all of these things are done, air sealing is done. Expanding foam is shot into every hole where a wire or pipe runs through a board, around window and door frames, and in any other place where outside air might sneak in.

Finally the batts of insulation that have been quietly waiting in huge piles are placed between the studs, into narrow nooks and crannies, and around the wire and electrical boxes. Dust masks and long sleeve shirts during this work lessen the itch factor.

The attic insulation is more difficult. It is done after the drywall is finished. A crew of two volunteers use a hopper with a blower and long hose to get the material into the attic. One person opens the sacks of material and dumps them into the hopper. The other person is in the attic with the hose crouching on the rat boards and spraying the insulation to every far corner to the right depth. It's a hot, sweaty, and itchy task so the workers trade off from time to time. Before that, on to covering the walls with drywall.

Sheet Rockin'

While the siding was being put up and the roof was being roofed, some things were happening inside the house. If it is a two-story home, the tubing for the radiant heating for the second level is installed by a few of the volunteers. This involves drilling holes in the joists so that the Pex tubing for the various heating zones can be snaked through. It's a time-consuming process involving volunteers as tubing unrollers, hole drillers, and tubing clampers along with putting in metal protectors where the tubing bends or might be punctured. The Pex tubing does have a unique feature in that it has a memory. That is, if kinked or unduly bent, applying heat will restore it to what it was before.

Somewhere along the way fiberglass tub and shower units arrived. These are big and bulky items that, while not heavy, don't go around tight corners. The idea is to get them into the house and into the bathrooms before so much is done that a tight fit may be too tight. The units can be moved to their final spots as the plumber finishes and before the drywalling is done. Occasionally it's necessary to remove a few wall studs to get them in. And it's best to be sure the drain and control valve end match where the plumbing will be installed before replacing any removed studs.

Then came the plumbers and electricians. There are habitat volunteers qualified to do these tasks in many situations but building codes and state regulations limit or prevent volunteers from doing them. By a licensed contractor doing the work, sometimes at no or reduced cost, it is done quickly and the project is now ready for the interior walls to be covered with wallboard aka drywall.

This gypsum-based material coated with heavy paper comes in one-half-inch and five-eighth-inch thicknesses four-feet-wide and either eight or twelve-feet-long. The one-half-inch material is normally used on the walls and the five-eighth thickness, being heavier, is destined for the ceilings. The shiny side goes out and the dull gray side goes in. The upper outside edge has a slight curve where the sheets join to aid in bedding the joint compound. There is also a green version of drywall called green board. This is used in places where moisture will be encountered such as in shower, tub, and laundry areas.

Drywalling is probably not one of the most favorite tasks for some volunteers as it involves heavy lifting and repetitive screwing or nailing. Unless a professional crew has volunteered to do it, we charge ahead. The ceiling of each room is done first. This involves lifting a sheet of material and holding it in place while drywall nails or screws are driven to hold it. Use of a portable lift makes this process easier. Each end must be on a supporting two-by-four nailing surface or meet in the center of a two-by-four. Ledger boards nailed to the top of the walls provide additional places to screw or nail.

Of course before the lift is used, holes need to be cut to fit over any light fixture openings or where a vent fan is installed. Or a rotozip tool is used to cut the opening when the drywall is in place. After the sheet is in place, it will be secured to the rafters with drywall nails or screws of appropriate length. The ceiling may call for one-and-five-eighths screws while walls may get one-and-one-half-inch screws.

Cutting the pieces to length before they are raised involves use of a drywall square to guide the scoring of the outer side of the panel. Then while standing it on edge from the backside, a knee is applied to the bigger part and the rest is bent in. The utility knife is then used to cut the remaining paper.

A similar process is used on the walls although there are many more openings for electrical outlets and switches to be cut out. The upper sheet goes up first. If you are lucky enough to be working alone, it is best to place a few large nails in the studs down forty-eight inches from the ceiling. This makes a place to rest the sheet on while getting the first nails or screws started. It is hard to hold up a sheet of drywall while reaching for a hammer or screwdriver. Drywall nails may be tacked in the sheet over studs so that a quick hammer tap can secure the sheet in place before it slips down.

The lower sheet is raised off the floor to butt against the upper sheet by using a lifter that is stepped on to raise the sheet. Drywall screws or nails are used in a designated spacing to fasten the sheet to the underlying studs. They must end up below the level of the drywall face but not puncture the paper surface.

When all the drywall is in place, the next step is called taping and texturing. Before that happens the floors are covered with Kraft paper taped in place. This saves untold hours of cleanup as what happens next is not a neat process. A swipe of joint compound is applied to each joint or seam, paper tape is imbedded in the compound, and more joint compound is applied over the paper. Metal edging is used under the compound around door openings. The mud is feathered out with a broad blade scraper to create a smooth transition. Corners have had the joint paper folded vertically before mudding.

Professionals don metal stilts to do the ceiling. Nail or screw heads are also mudded over. With one or more applications of the compound, drying, and sanding, a smooth surface emerges. After the final sanding, a texture coating is sprayed on. The entire process can take three or four days to complete during which time the area is off limits to volunteers if professionals are doing the work. Heaters are used to speed up the drying process. On our 2006 Blitz Build house drywalling, taping, texturing, and painting were done at night under lighting as the building process rolled on.

The Long
Count-Down

Now that the house has evolved into a place with identifiable rooms, the work goes from major tasks such as framing and siding to a mixture of efforts happening at many different places at the same time. Out in the utility-storage room, the main power panel has been installed and connected to the electric line to the property. Soon some of the electrical outlets will be 'live' and usable. Near the breaker box a 'smart' panel is in place to route the telephone and cable lines. A heating manifold for the radiant heating system is a sculpture of copper pipes and valves mounted on one wall. The two hot water heaters (domestic and heating) are mounted on platforms and ready to be connected. Overflow pipes from the tanks to the outside will be fitted, glued, and run out through the wall.

Inside the house a crew is busy installing the interior doors on newly installed jambs. The doors will probably be taken off and away for final painting. Outside the entry doors, work is being done on the porches if they are part of the plan. Concrete slabs have been framed and poured. After a corner post is set in place in a bracket in the concrete, two four-by-twelve beams placed from the corner post back to the house walls and mounted in hanging brackets. These and the supporting post will be boxed in. HardiePlank™ paneling will be installed and trimmed out.

The ongoing background music, to all that happens from now until the dedication of the house, is the sound of brushes and rollers as painting in one area or another goes on. Introductory notes were heard when the soffit sheets were painted just as the roof trusses were being installed. The panels are nailed in place under the eaves just after the sub-fascia and fascia are finished. The fascia could also be painted. When the drywall is finished, the interior walls are painted before the paper over the slab is removed. At the same time on or off site, the material for the interior trim is being painted. It will be painted and touched up again as the house is finished. The outside corner trim gets painted before the siding gets installed and again later. Exterior siding is caulked and painted. The music of the rollers and brushes won't stop until just before the cleanup crew arrives, often just before dedication day. And, as finished as the house looks from outside, the inside needs a little more work.

Floored

This is the time in the project when heavy four-foot-long boxes of laminate flooring arrive on site. We use the snap-together laminate rather than the edge glue type. The material needs to sit at room temperature for a few days to acclimate to its' new home before it is installed. Then, over two or three work days, it will be installed in much of the house by teams of two or three volunteers spending most of their time in prayerful positions.

The first decision is what direction to lay the floor so that it is in sync with closets, door openings, hallways, and people installing the material in other rooms. Then the floors are swept and vacuumed so that no debris is left to lift the flooring. After that, a thin foam sheet is laid out over the slab in three-foot increments. This insulates the laminate from the slab and cushions it. The floor will be a 'floating floor' which means that the entire interlocked floor can expand and contract under the baseboards that are installed later.

Tools needed are a tape measure, speed square, pencil, special hard rubber tapping blocks to make the joints tight, and knee pads. There is also a metal bar with the ends at right angles to use to pull ends lengthwise as needed. The basic process is to select pieces from the box that pattern match somewhat where they join. Lengthwise each piece has a thin and a wide interlocking edge. Wide and thin lock together. Each end is also different. This is important to remember as the floor is laid and some ends are cut off. Save them.

The pieces for a row are laid end to end along the starting wall even with the drywall. One piece is left flat and the joining piece is tilted slightly lengthwise, precisely lined up end to end, and lowered so that it blends seamlessly with the other. Hopefully. If not, lift carefully and try again. When the wall is reached, a piece will have to be saw cut to finish the row. This is where cutting off the correct end is critical. Save the cut off piece as, guess what, it may be usable at the far end of the next row.

When one row is down and joined, the next row is laid out. Avoid any matching cross seams by eight inches or more. After the row is laid parallel to the prior row and ends joined, the team tilts the entire row and joins it to the joint in the prior row. When it matches all along the line, it is lowered forward and down into place with hand pushing and palm pounding. Be careful not to chip the thin interlocking edge. If necessary, the rubber block is used to tighten the joint, and the metal tool to pull lengthwise. Row after row is added in the same way.

When a wall, closet, or door opening is encountered, cut and fit carefully. A small handsaw or an electric jigsaw is used for these cuts. The final row next to a wall or in a closet may have to be cut lengthwise to fit properly. Any minor cutting errors will be covered by the baseboard trim. Large ones will not be. The door openings may have an open space left where a threshold molding will be installed.

While all this is happening, another team is ensconced in the bathroom or kitchen working with ceramic tile. This work starts by placing cement board over the slab or sub-floor. The board has lines that can be used to guide in placing the tile. Careful calculations are made so that the tile can start at the center of the area and not end up with an awkward narrow strip next to a tub or wall. Thinset mortar is mixed and troweled onto a small area of the floor using a trowel with a toothed edge. A square of tile is carefully laid into the mortar and gently pressed down.

The next tile is placed with plastic spacers used along each adjoining edge. They will be removed after the mortar has hardened. Metal leveling bars (levels without a bubble) are used to be sure the tiles are level with each other. Pieces that need to be trimmed to size are cut on a special tile saw. This saw has a diamond blade that is water cooled and a slide to guide the tile through at the correct angle.

After the tile is set in place and the thinset hardened, the spacers are pried out and the joints cleaned using a special tool. The joints will now be grouted using a grout color-matched to the tile. This turns out to be a labor-intensive time-critical process as the grout compound has a specified open time to be used. The grout is troweled across the tile in stages and down into the joints. After a series of joints are filled, the remaining grout needs to be cleaned off of the tile surface. This is done with large wet sponges that are constantly wrung out in the bucket of water which has to be replaced quite often. Two or three more cleanings of the tile are done to remove the haze left by the grout.

The Final Push

As the flooring is finished, there is a new sense of urgency on the site. It's not a race to the finish line but an urgent effort to protect the new floor while the last thousand or so trips are made in and out while the interior work is being done over several weeks. All sawing is done outside. If the floors are not protected by drop cloths, shoe covers are worn when inside. Or shoes are left at the door. Lunch may be done outside or in another house.

Baseboard trim is one of the first steps at this phase. It has been painted and will be painted some more after cutting, installing, and filling of finish nail holes. The trim goes along every lower wall base (baseboard!) except where a cabinet, shower, or other impediment exists. It fits flush with door trim and may be mitered at some corners for a precise fit. It should be close to the floor with no high or low spots that are obvious. Nailing is done with finish nails usually using a brad nailer. If the studs can be found (every sixteen inches), they should be nailed into.

Trim is also placed around the outside of every inside door opening. The vertical sides may be mitered at forty-five degrees to match the top piece or squared depending on the house plans. Window ledges have special wide trim pieces that may extend past the window opening. A decorative piece of trim may be installed under these.

In each closet, ledger boards are now cut to length and installed on the ends and back. These are nailed through the drywall into the backer blocks installed much earlier or into the studs.

A shelf is cut from melamine board and fitted over the ledger board. Then a piece of trim about nine inches long is centered and nailed vertically down from the back ledger. This supports a bracket that supports the shelf. It also supports the wooden hanging rod as it runs the length of the closet to rest in end supports. Storage closets get a similar treatment but may not have a hanging rod and may have more shelves.

Along with the shelving work, bifold doors are installed. This starts with installing a metal track on the center line of the closet entry. The door top wheels will run in the track to open and fold or close and unfold. The fixed end of each door fits top and bottom with spring-loaded pivot pieces going into adjustable brackets. Where the sweat is expended is in trying to have the door meet at the center evenly while also spaced properly at the far ends. If the door opening is not square and the proper width, some frustration can result. After the proper spacing is finally achieved, guide pieces are screwed to the inside leading edge of each door to keep them even when closed.

At this point volunteers who have been narrowly focused on their tasks might look around and realize what else has been happening. The blue boxes with the wires coming out have been transformed into electrical outlets, cable and telephone outlets, and wall switches. Wall plates now hide the blue and gray boxes. Overhead light fixtures have magically appeared. The hanging light over the dining area is tied up high so that it won't be walked into for the fifth time.

While this is noticed, kitchen cabinets and bathroom vanities arrive and need to be placed after being sorted as to location. Upper cabinets are fairly easy to separate from base units but sequence needs to be established as to what goes where. A diagram that should be with the delivery can help. The base unit for the sink will need to have holes cut in the back for plumbing entry and exit. The units will be leveled and shimmed as needed before adjoining units are fastened together and screwed to the wall.

A level line is struck on the back wall where the upper units will rest. A ledger board might be used at this step to support the cabinet units as they are placed. If the blocking was done properly, the back of each unit will be screwed in tightly to it. Drywall alone will not hold the weight of upper cabinets and their contents. Each adjoining unit is edge-screwed to the prior unit. Doors are reinstalled and aligned. Bathroom vanities are base units only and are quickly installed. Sink openings are traced and cut in the kitchen and bathroom countertops. Now the Formica people can be called and the countertops finished in the color and pattern selected by the homeowner.

Before the kitchen sink and bathroom basins are installed, the faucets are installed. This simple step prevents much grousing and gnashing of teeth as the assembled units can be dropped in complete without trying to do the work from under the counter. Next is toilet assembly and placement. The tank is carefully attached to the seat and the tank float installed. The completed assembly is carefully set in place over the hold down bolts and wax ring sealer. The plastic plug that keeps stuff out of the toilet drain pipe during construction should be removed before this is done. Hold down bolts are carefully tightened. The shower gets a control valve and a shower head. Water supply lines for the toilets, basins, and kitchen sink are added, the water supply turned on, and a check is made for any leaks. The water level in the toilet tanks is adjusted.

If towel bars, toilet paper holders, and related hardware were not installed earlier, that will be done next. Then putting up mirrors or medicine cabinets will complete the work.

In the kitchen, holes have been cut in a cabinet top and bottom and a sheet-metal microwave vent has been placed. This is concealed from sight as a wood surround is built and placed between the cabinet top and the ceiling. If the microwave has arrived it will be mounted on a special mounting plate above the space for the stove.

If it has not happened sooner, a delivery truck arrives with the stove and refrigerator. These units are donated by Whirlpool to every new Habitat house. The dishwasher and microwave have been donated by the locally-owned Sears store. With the installation of these items, it's time to look around and see what needs to still be done. Cabinet knobs and drawer pulls selected by the homeowner need to be put on. A special template guides the drilling of the holes for these. Any toe boards that were not placed earlier are cut and placed. The counters need to be cleared so that a tile back splash can be placed. This is sometimes done on the morning of the dedication as other last minute punch list items are checked off. A cleanup crew of volunteers arrives on the last Saturday and thoroughly cleans the house. The construction door locks are replaced with the homeowner door locks and the keys turned over to the site supervisor. With that step, the volunteers have completed their work. Last minute landscape work is done outside as the builders finally yield to the efforts to prepare for the dedication.

Aloha Again

Wednesday, January 9, 2008. Our last day working inside on the final house at the Campbell Street Habitat For Humanity Project. It's nice not to be working outside in the intermittent rain though it is a warm enough winter day in Port Angeles. We complete punch-list items and look for things not on the list. The site supervisor has just called for the final building inspection. Passing that plus getting a certificate of occupancy will make it possible for the new homeowner and her family to move in. For them it is the end of months of waiting, working, and hoping as they now start a new journey. For the volunteers on the project it is the point where the journey starts again.

This stage on a Habitat project, when all the homes are completed, is not unlike a very friendly divorce proceeding. It's been a good relationship between the volunteers and the families but now it's time to go our separate ways. The volunteers have worked month after month alongside the families who are putting in their hours of sweat equity as they help their houses take shape. There have been good and not-so-good work days as a common goal has been sought. They have shared workday lunches and labored long hours together as the renters of sometimes marginal housing transcended to becoming owners of their own homes. Now the families will have the keys to the homes and we others are out of their new spaces. If we have to go inside to make a final door or trim adjustment we will have to knock first. When the rain stops there is final landscape and fence work to do outside along with site cleanup and construction trailer moving. Except for those tasks, the builders are taking their tools and moving on.

This four-home project started in June, 2006 with a one-week Blitz Build of the first house. The goal was for professional homebuilders and their crews to build one house in one week from the slab up. Volunteers were there to support the effort. Materials from stacks of lumber to siding and paint were on site in readiness for the effort. Some items were donated, some were bought. After the parade of professionals moved on, the volunteers added the finishing touches and then moved on to the other three houses including one financed by Thrivent Thrift and built by Lutherans from area churches and Habitat volunteers.

At noon we gather inside this last house to sit on plastic lawn chairs and share a lunch provided for us by a board member who will also be leading the cleaning crew this weekend. It's a very hearty homemade chicken noodle soup, homemade bread, and still warm cookies. Food like that will guarantee that long-time volunteers will appear at the next project. We swap 'war stories' of events and people involved along the way in getting to this point. Then back to the final tasks on the punch-list. Time to replace the construction locks with the homeowner locks. Clear the floors and counters of tools and supplies. And look around at all that has been done over the months as this house now becomes a home. Then we sign out and slowly start to leave, one or two at a time, to go our separate ways. Some of us will work for a few weeks fifty miles down the road on the Forks project. Most of the die-hard volunteers will meet again at the next project when it gets underway. And, like old soldiers, some will fade away and be remembered as the next project unfolds.

There will also be new volunteers and oncoming family members as the process starts again. We may see the Campbell Street family members at another site or around town but they now go forward into their new lives. We old-timers fondly remember the family from the Maizie Court project in Sequim that drove to Port Angeles to bring us homemade cookies. And David, a teenager from that project who continued to volunteer in Port Angeles when his school work allowed. Every project adds to the inventory of memories.

Now the last day ends with volunteers gone and a family moving in, we know that most of us will meet as the process starts again. And those not there will be remembered as part of our Habitat family history.

Dedication Day

The final event for each home or group of homes is the dedication of each house. Somehow between the time the volunteers leave on Saturday and 2 p.m. Sunday, other things happen. More landscaping appears, if not in final form. A shelter tent may be put up. Rows of folding chairs appear along with tables of cake and other goodies. Coffee, hot chocolate and soft drinks are on board. The new homeowners, family members, relatives and friends arrive. Board and committee members not often seen on site are present. A clergy person is present for each family if more than one house is to be dedicated. Many of the volunteers are present with their spouses who support them in their being away from home during retirement.

The ceremony starts with a welcome and introductions by the chapter president. A prayer is followed by opening remarks by the affiliate executive director. Board members are introduced. Volunteer efforts are noted. Each home to be dedicated is consecrated by a pastor from the homeowner's church. Then the family or families step forward one group at a time, are introduced, and invited to say a few words. Each of our family members is presented a quilt made by the Sunbonnet Sue Quilt Club of Sequim and a small bookcase made by shop students at Sequim High School. Among the donated books is a new Bible for each family. Then the key to the new home is presented.

After all the homes have been dedicated, and the keys and the Bible presented, a closing prayer is followed by a ribbon cutting. Then the homes are open for touring by the guests along with sharing of refreshments. Later, while the shelter, tables and chairs are being removed, the family, or families, start moving in to their new home and life.

Epilog

On June 25, 2008, eight of us meet in Port Angeles to work on the next Habitat house. This home is being financed by Thrivent Thrift, a Lutheran group, and built by volunteers from area Lutheran churches along with Habitat. The walls are being framed and raised with Dick Chambers guiding this part of the project. Terry Reichart, Paul La Marche, and Pete Jensen, part of the Bell Hill Gang, are there. Chuck Lamb arrives later. Jon Fager and Lynn Drake join in the framing work. Russ Holt and I are assigned to unraveling the jumble of items in the forty-foot shipping container tool shed and storage area that has just been moved on site. We listen to the litany of the safety lecture and move on to our tasks. Like Yogi said, déjà vu all over again.

Term Limits

Backers: Two-by-four or two-by-six blocks between studs behind the drywall for the attachment of cabinets, closet shelf supports, shower enclosures, stair rails and so forth.

Barge Boards: Also called fascia. These are the long two-by-six boards along the truss ends. They are the outside part of the eaves.

Bird Blocks: Two-by-four pieces set on edge on the top plates between trusses to keep birds out. Some have holes covered by wire mesh for attic ventilation.

Brick Molding: The wood around the door jamb over to the OSB.

Burning (an inch): Not a fire. Starting a tape measurement at the one-inch mark to get an accurate measurement. The inch must be added to the far end or the board will be short an inch.

Cat's Paw: A small nail removal bar that resembles a cat's paw.

Caulk: The (usually) silicone stuff applied with a caulking gun to fill in gaps in siding, around showers and tubs, and other places where a joint is visible. The tip of the tube must be cut off at the appropriate exit diameter and at an angle before puncturing the inner seal that can't be seen.

Diagonals: Corner to opposite corner measurements to confirm that a rectangle or square really is.

Duplex Nails: Nails with a second head above the first one so that they can be easily pulled out from forms that are not to be fastened forever.

Eaves: Roof overhang back to the side of the house.

Face Nailing: Nailing straight? into the surface of a board.

Factory Edge: The so-far uncut edge of a piece of material which should be straight. On OSB, it is colored.

Fascia: See 'Barge Board'

Footings: The lower and wider part of a foundation that supports the weight of the structure.

Hangers: Metal brackets of various shapes and sizes used where boards join at angles and where extra support and strength is needed. i.e.: joist hanger.

Hard Hat: Hard plastic safety hat worn most of the time on site to protect head from falling objects dropped from above or that should not have been on the top of a step ladder.

HardiePlank™: Proprietary term for a cement and fiber composite used as exterior siding.

Headers: Pieces of two-by material in various widths that go above door and window framing to fill the opening and provide added strength.

Hurricane Clips: Metal clips nailed between the trusses and the top plates to hold the house frame to the roof if high winds are encountered. They are nailed using fourteen Tico™ nails each. Some are two-piece and marked 'L' or 'R' (left or right) for proper installation.

Jambs: The frame around a door.

Joists, Rim and otherwise: The two-by-six or wider beams that span an open space from side to side. Rim joists are on edge around the perimeter of a foundation.

Laminate Flooring: Snap-together or glue-together composite flooring.

Lookouts: Wooden brackets installed to support a roof overhang.

Miter: Angle of a Bishop's hat. Cutting at forty-five degree angles for a tight-fitting corner.

Mortising: 1. A method of joining wood. 2. Cutting into wood for a special purpose, such as a door striker plate.

Nails: Pointed metal things with a flat head (except for brad or finish nails) in various diameters and lengths and coatings that are pounded in to hold pieces of wood together. Traditionally sold by weight per hundred; now indicates length and diameter. Don't use a sixteen-penny sinker as a four-penny finishing nail.

Nail Set: Not two nails. A short metal punch-like tool used to drive brads and finishing nails below the surface so that caulk or wood putty can fill the hole which will then be painted over and presumably invisible.

Oriented Strand Board (OSB): Material used for sheathing and other purposes. Made of wood chips 'oriented' in a direction to give strength and rigidity.

Palm Nailer: Small air-powered palm-held nailer used for nailing in difficult places.

Pex: Tubing used in a radiant heating system.

Plate Compactor: Not for kitchen use. A powered tamper or vibrator used to compact fill material such as dirt or rock.

Plates - Sole, Base, Upper, and Top: The two -by-four or two-by-six board that lies flat and forms the top and bottom of the wall framing.

Plumb Bob: Totally Bob. A pointed weight on a string used to find out if something is vertical.

Pressure-Treated Lumber: Lumber treated with a preservative and used where it is in contact with the slab or foundation.

Radiant Heating: Heating system where hot water is circulated through tubing under the floor to warm the house.

Rat Boards: Long one-by-four or other boards, usually side-by-side, nailed down in the attic over rafters so that a worker can crawl around without falling through the drywall.

Ram Set: Special tool used to fire nails into concrete to anchor interior walls.

Reciprocating Saw: Long, heavy power saw with an extended blade that goes back and forth (reciprocates) to cut out openings and for flush cuts in places where other saws do not care to go. Can cut wood, metal, and plastic with the proper blade.

Roofing: The shingles or other material laid down as a roof covering.

Roofing Felt: The felt is the black cloth that goes under the roofing shingles.

Roofing Paper: The newer material that has replaced roofing felt.

Router: High-speed power tool using various bits to cut out window openings, shape edges, and perform other exotic tasks.

Running The Corners: See 'Diagonals'.

Safety Glasses: Clear plastic goggles worn to protect eyes from dust and flying objects such a nails, wood chips, and chisel pieces.

Saws: Hand or electric-powered tools for cutting wood and other materials.

Screeding: Using a long board to level and smooth cement or fill material.

Squares - Carpenters, Combination, Speed, Drywall: Device for making sure corners are square and marking lines at right or forty-five degree angles across material. The small speed square is the most common and easy to carry and use. It is not square but rather a right-angle triangle. The combination square is one step up and has a measuring blade that slides through a handle that has forty-five and ninety-degree angles. It may also have a bubble level and an awl for marking. A Carpenter's Square has two sides at a right angle to each other and varies in length of the sides. It is used in framing and in stair building. The largest square is the drywall square used for measuring and cutting drywall. It has a handle that fits along the top of the drywall and a four-foot blade to guide measuring and scoring of the material.

Stem Walls: Inside foundation walls that are formed on top of the footings.

Stress Panel: A full OSB sheet at a corner.

Studs - King, Jack, and Cripples: The two-by-four or two-by-six pieces that are the vertical pieces used in framing walls. The king studs are on the outsides of door and window openings. A jack stud is a shorter stud on the inside of a king stud and supports the crosspiece for the header. A cripple is a short vertical stud under window framing.

Stud Finder: An electronic tool used to possibly locate studs under drywall when nailing or screwing something into the stud. Accuracy is at times questionable.

Tico™ Nails: Short, fat nail used to nail joist hangers and hurricane clips in place.

Toenail: Angle nailing when other ways don't work due to space or other limits. The nail is started straight and then tilted to forty-five degrees as it goes deeper. Then another nail is driven from the opposite side to bring the wood back to where it should be.

Trusses: The engineered wood structures that span the house under the roof and give a slope to the roof.

Wonder Bar: A wide metal pry bar used to remove nails when the claw on the hammer is ineffective. Also used as a wrecking bar to separate pieces nailed together. Can also be used as a drywall lifter.

Notes:

Notes:

Notes:

Notes:

Notes:

Notes:

Notes:

Notes:

Notes:

Notes:

Notes:

Notes:

Notes:

Notes:

Order Form

Old Red Barn Publishing
P.O. Box 921
Sequim, Washington 98382
360.582.1598

Qty	Item	Price	Total
	The Road North Tales of an Urban Sourdough	**19.95** Canada 23.95	
	The Photo Op	19.95 Canada 23.95	
	HABITATIN' FOR HUMANITY	9.95 Canada 12.95	
		Book Total	
		Postage & Handling: 3.95 per book	
		Washington Residents: Please add 8.4% sales Tax	
		Grand Total	

Payment must accompany order.
Please make checks payable to **Old Red Barn Publishing.**

Name _____

Address _____

City _____ State _____ Zip _____

Phone _____

Order Form

Old Red Barn Publishing
P.O. Box 921
Sequim, Washington 98382
360.582.1598

Qty	Item	Price	Total
	The Road North Tales of an Urban Sourdough	**19.95** **Canada 23.95**	
	The Photo Op	19.95 Canada 23.95	
	HABITATIN' FOR HUMANITY	9.95 Canada 12.95	
		Book Total	
		Postage & Handling: 3.95 per book	
		Washington Residents: Please add 8.4% sales Tax	
		Grand Total	

Payment must accompany order.
Please make checks payable to **Old Red Barn Publishing**.

Name _____

Address _____

City _____ State _____ Zip _____

Phone _____

Order Form

Old Red Barn Publishing
P.O. Box 921
Sequim, Washington 98382
360.582.1598

Qty	Item	Price	Total
	The Road North Tales of an Urban Sourdough	**19.95** Canada 23.95	
	The Photo Op	19.95 Canada 23.95	
	HABITATIN' FOR HUMANITY	9.95 Canada 12.95	
		Book Total	
		Postage & Handling: 3.95 per book	
		Washington Residents: Please add 8.4% sales Tax	
		Grand Total	

Payment must accompany order.
Please make checks payable to **Old Red Barn Publishing**.

Name _____

Address _____

City _____ State _____ Zip _____

Phone _____

www.ingramcontent.com/pod-product-compliance
Lightning Source LLC
Chambersburg PA
CBHW022121280326
41933CB00007B/493